Some birds **poop** fifty times a day! That's a lot of **poop**!

Snake **poop** is smelly.

Some fish eat whale **poop**!

Jellyfish **poop** from their mouth. That's weird!

Whale **poop** can be **pink**.

Turtles **poop** while they swim.

Some animals live in the water.
Do they **poop** too? Yes, even animals
that live in the water **poop**.

Do animals in cold places **poop**? Yes, they do!

Birds **poop** in the sky.
"Watch out below!"

"I **poop**
on the potty!"

Seal **poop** is stinky!
It smells like fish.

Pets **poop**! Where do they **poop**?

Fish make loooong **poops** in their bowls!

Birds **poop** in their cages.
A litter box is a purr-fect place for a cat to **poop**.
"I **poop** on the potty!"
Bunnies make lots of **poops**! Time for a **poop** scoop.

Do people you know **poop**? Yes, they do!

Grown-ups **poop**!
Teachers **poop.** Parents **poop.**
Crossing guards **poop**!
Bus drivers **poop**!
STOP
SCHOOL
"I **poop**
on the potty!"

There is even **poop** in space!

Have you ever seen a potty constellation?

Astronauts **poop**!

Someday, humans might **poop** on another planet!

Hmm, what does alien **poop** look like?

Do people and animals in Fairyland **poop?**
Yes, they do!

Dragons need **lots** of toilet paper.

Gnome **poop** is very small.

Unicorns make **rainbow poop!**

What's that smell from under the bridge?!

A witch's cat **poops** wherever it wants.
Fairy **poop** sparkles!
HOME SWEET HOME
"I **poop** on the potty!"

Do you know who else **poops**?
Me! I **poop** on the potty!

Wiping keeps your bottom clean.

Soap and water make your hands clean. Being clean keeps you healthy.